T0129984

Achieve the
Dream
- Your Own Home

Anita Marshall

BALBOA.
PRESS
A DIVISION OF HAY HOUSE

Balboa Press books may be ordered through booksellers or by contacting:

Balboa Press
A Division of Hay House
1663 Liberty Drive
Bloomington, IN 47403
www.balboapress.com.au
1 (877) 407-4847

Because of the dynamic nature of the Internet, any web addresses or
links contained in this book may have changed since publication and
may no longer be valid. The views expressed in this work are solely those
of the author and do not necessarily reflect the views of the publisher,
and the publisher hereby disclaims any responsibility for them.

The author of this book does not dispense medical advice or prescribe the use
of any technique as a form of treatment for physical, emotional, or medical
problems without the advice of a physician, either directly or indirectly. The
intent of the author is only to offer information of a general nature to help
you in your quest for emotional and spiritual well-being. In the event you use
any of the information in this book for yourself, which is your constitutional
right, the author and the publisher assume no responsibility for your actions.

Any people depicted in stock imagery provided by Thinkstock are
models, and such images are being used for illustrative purposes only.
Certain stock imagery © Thinkstock.

Print information available on the last page.

ISBN: 978-1-5043-0450-4 (sc)
ISBN: 978-1-5043-0451-1 (e)

Balboa Press rev. date: 09/22/2016

Acknowledgements

I am truly blessed to have wonderful people in my life who encourage me to follow my dreams and who believe in me.

I would firstly like to thank my son, Blake, who has inspired me to be the best person I can be through his encouragement and honesty.

My parents, Rhonda and David, who have given me so much encouragement in all my business ventures. I am very blessed to have such positive, supportive parents.

My wonderful staff at Advanced Finance Solutions who help me so much with all of our projects, including this book. They have read this book so many times they almost know it word for word and are probably very glad to see the final edition in print! Thank you Marion Reid, Taylah Insole, Donella Whiteman, Leigh Watson, Prue Upton, Leesa Bigham and Zoe McKenna.

I am truly grateful to all of our wonderful clients who have put their faith in us to help them on the path to buying their own home. It is so rewarding to work with people who have been renting for so long and are able to get into the home of their dreams.

Thanks to all of our followers and friends on social media who have helped us to spread the word that home ownership is possible. Your support is greatly appreciated.

Thanks also to Ian Pugh for editing and proofreading this book.

And, last but not least, I would like to say thank you to "property" in general, as that has been the tool that has helped me achieve financial success in many ways.

Anita

Contents

INTRODUCTION

Let me guess - you dream about owning your own home one day but at the moment it seems completely out of reach. If that sounds like you then let me first say that you are not alone. In fact, in this day and age, more and more people are looking at the housing market and wondering how on earth they will ever manage to get their foot in the door (their *own* door!)

Over the past few years, I have come across some alarming statistics that reveal the number of people renting who have given up on their dreams of ever owning their own home. This is something that makes me really sad.

The most recent research, funded by the Australian Government for *The Household, Income and Labour Dynamics in Australia (HILDA) Survey*, has revealed that home ownership numbers have declined in the past few years to an alarmingly low figure.

There have also been a lot of foreign investors buying real estate in Australia, pushing up the price of our real estate and, as a result, pushing our own Aussie buyers out of the market, especially in some of our capital cities.

Thankfully, new lending regulations for foreign buyers have slowed down the foreign investor market, which has led to an ease in the sharp rise in house prices.

We have also seen a surge in petitions and groups opposed to foreign ownership in our country.

I believe that the best way to get around this problem is to get MORE Australians buying their own homes. I'm also convinced that the best to approach this issue is from a proactive and positive angle.

Property has been very good to me over the years. I have bought and sold quite a number of properties and every single one has contributed to my wealth creation.

There are a lot of different investments available to us but what I love about property is: -

- **It's easy to understand**. Despite having a Diploma in Financial Planning, I still wouldn't like to be choosing my investments in shares or managed funds as this requires a high level of research and a constant eye on the market. Even then, there are a lot of other factors you need to be aware of in today's rapidly changing world financial climate. It makes sense to leave these decisions to the experts who work in that industry on a full-time basis. Property, on the other hand, is relatively simple.

- **You can easily do your own research**. You can jump online to any of the real estate sites and work out average house prices, see what has sold, what is for sale and then start looking. It doesn't take long to be able to recognise a good buy.
- **You can borrow a higher percentage on property than most other investments.** A lot of the mortgage providers will lend 95% (or more) on a residential property which means you can get into the property market with a fairly low deposit.
- **You can live in your property** while it is growing in value. You can't live in a share! Why not be paying off your own home instead of someone else's? You may as well be contributing to your own wealth creation rather than that of your landlord!
- **Property is generally a stable investment** – most properties grow in value even in difficult financial climates. People will always need somewhere to live so housing is always going to be an asset that people will need. In my opinion, property is a reasonably predictable and stable investment.
- **It's considered the "Great Australian Dream"** – it feels great to own a part of our amazing country and to own something you can call "home" in Australia. The more Aussies doing this the better.

Despite how impossible it may seem to you at the moment, I assure you that your dream is achievable. Success in home ownership doesn't come by accident though. What you do need is the right attitude, some good ideas, a positive approach, some discipline and a better understanding of how it all works. Then you can develop a "plan".

If this sounds appealing, I encourage you to read this book. I'm confident that some of the insights, tips and hints shared in these pages will help make your dream a reality.

Please help spread the word that home ownership for Australians in Australia is possible.

Let's keep the dream alive!

Anita Marshall

CHAPTER 1

THE DEPOSIT
- YES, YOU CAN!

Your biggest obstacle to owning your own home and probably the question you ask yourself the most is "How am I ever going to get a deposit together?" You're probably paying rent (and rents are high) and you just can't see a way of saving at the same time.

Firstly, let me say that if this is how you're feeling then you're definitely not alone! In fact, this is the No 1 problem that people have when they come and see me for help.

I know that it can feel completely overwhelming and impossible but trust me there is a way. So I'm going to start by giving you some information about three possible ways that you can achieve this.

OPTION 1: THE FAMILY GUARANTEE

More often than not, family love to help others members of their family if they think they can. This is especially true for parents or other close family when it comes to helping their children or other close family get out of the rental market and into their own homes.

Some might be willing but may not realise they are in a position to help. They may think they have to stand as guarantors for your entire loan, which can discourage some parents/family from being involved. Years ago if a family member went guarantor on a home loan they were required to guarantee the entire loan. However, it's not like that anymore (thank goodness). So it's definitely worth having the conversation because if they are willing to help there could be a way.

If you have a family member with equity in their own home, then they might be willing to go guarantor for a portion of your loan. They are not required to take out the loan in their name or to go onto the title of the property you are buying. It is simply a guarantee on a portion of the loan with the equity in their property as security on your home loan.

Usually they guarantee around 20%-25% of the property purchase price (not the whole loan). This can usually be released as soon as you have at least 10% equity in your property through doing a refinance of the loan to release the family guarantee.

Generally, the person guaranteeing the loan needs to be related to the borrower in some way. Often this is parents, grandparents, aunties, uncles, siblings, etc.

The family guarantee means you don't need to save a deposit at all as it allows you to borrow the full purchase price plus costs associated with the purchase.

This option also reduces some of the fees associated with the loan. For example, Lenders Mortgage Insurance is not payable when you are using a family guarantee.

The family member does need to understand that they are a "security" guarantor on the loan. This means that if you don't make the payments on the home and there is a mortgagee in possession sale of the home by the bank or lender, then the family member may be required to cover any shortfall after the sale of your home up to the value of the guarantee. The full terms and conditions of a family guarantee are given to the family member prior to signing the agreement so that they fully understand the guarantee. It is highly recommended that they seek legal advice so that they fully understand their obligations of the family guarantee.

The banks/lenders still require you to be able to afford the repayments so you will still be required to buy a property within your means. The lenders won't allow you to buy a property that you cannot afford as that would not be responsible lending.

Not all of the banks/lenders give this option so it is worth speaking to a broker to explore the lender options available to you.

OPTION 2: GIFTED FUNDS

If there is someone in your family that genuinely wants to help, then they might prefer to consider gifting you a portion of the deposit you require. Again, it's worth talking to them and mentioning the amount you need for the deposit. Even receiving just a portion of it could make all the difference.

If they agree to gift you a portion of the deposit required, it is possible (depending on the lender) for the family member to retain the funds in their own account until the time of settlement. For example, if you have 5% of the purchase price in your own savings account which has been genuinely saved by you (or been in your account for at least 3 months) then the family member can usually just provide a statutory declaration stating that they are gifting you the remainder of the funds needed (usually another 5%-8%) then only hand those funds over at the time of settlement. Knowing this is an option may make the difference.

If they are gifting you the full 10%-13% (5% deposit on the property price plus enough to cover stamp duty and legal fees - this generally adds up to another 5-8%) it will need to go into a bank account in your name (or into a joint account in their name and your name if they are more comfortable with that). With most lenders, that money will have to sit there for 3 months. This is designed to prove that you can hold the funds in your account for at least 3 months without touching it.

There are one or two lenders currently allowing you to have it there for less than 3 months but then the rest of the loan application would need to be very strong to get an approval through.

OPTION 3: SAVING THE DEPOSIT

I know it's hard but sometimes you need to make sacrifices in order to reach your goal. Every cent you can save can go towards the deposit on your home. It might take a few years to save up enough but it will be well worth it in the long run.

When I was 22 years of age (seems like yesterday) I was engaged and keen to buy a home with my fiancé. Back then you needed at least 20% deposit for a home plus enough to cover stamp duty, legal fees, etc. To enable us to achieve our dream of our first home we bought a very basic caravan for $1400 and put that in my brother-in-law's backyard in Cardiff (a suburb of Newcastle in NSW). We lived in that caravan for 18 months while we saved for our first home and it actually turned out to be a fun time. We had parties in the annexe with friends on weekends (instead of going out) and generally saved every cent we could.

Living in a caravan in winter is a very, very good incentive for saving! We also spent a lot of time at my parent's place in Port Stephens, which was great for a bit of luxury but both of us were keen to get into our own home as quickly as possible. We took on second jobs to bring in the extra cash required to accelerate our savings plan. I worked at night teaching at a local TAFE college and my fiancé fixed up old or damaged cars and sold them to boost the savings.

It proved to me that you can be happy no matter where you are living. I still have fond memories of some of the parties and fun we had in the caravan. Going without for a while also gives you a greater appreciation when there is more abundance in your life.

So, the moral of my story is that getting to where you want to be, may mean going without for a little while. This might mean putting a hold on your social life or not buying the latest phone or items for your wardrobe. You may have to cancel shopping expeditions and holidays for a while but it WILL be worth it. When you are saving towards something as important as your own home it makes it a little easier to go without the luxuries for a while.

CHAPTER 2

THE HOME OWNERSHIP FINANCE PLAN

If you are going to have to save the deposit you will need a budget or as I prefer to call it – **The Home Ownership Finance Plan.**

Having a Home Ownership Finance Plan will enable you to work out how much you can spend and save each time you are paid.

I recommend 3 savings accounts as follows: -

Account Number 1 - Home ownership savings account.

Put as much as you can into this account every week. This account is where your savings for your home will accumulate and ideally, you shouldn't touch this account until you are ready to put the deposit down on your home.

Account Number 2 - Bills account

Work out a total of all your expenses and put this amount aside every week into your Bills account. This way, when a bill arrives, you will have enough to cover it. Remember to include all your expenses, for example:

- phone
- mobile
- internet
- electricity
- water usage
- gas
- rent
- gym membership
- sport
- education expenses
- insurances
- car rego, insurances, maintenance, repairs
- HECS/HELP payments
- lay-bys, store cards, credit cards, personal loans (ideally you need to get rid of as many of these as you can before applying for your home loan)
- any other expense (look back over the last 12 months and add every expense you can think of)

Work out how much these items cost you on a weekly basis and then put that amount into the account every single time you are paid. If you are paid fortnightly or monthly then work out the figures fortnightly or monthly.

For example, if you know your car rego, insurance, tyres, maintenance, green slip, etc. will cost you $1500 a year then put aside $29 per week into your bills account so that when these things are due you already have the money available and don't have to dip into your home ownership savings.

Account 3 - Spending account

Work out how much you are going to allow yourself to spend on: -

- groceries
- food
- alcohol
- clothes
- shoes
- medical /pharmaceutical supplies
- going out
- takeaway meals
- lunches
- petrol
- dinners out
- laundry/dry cleaning
- hair care
- holidays
- newspapers
- magazines
- Christmas and birthday presents
- Any other type of expenses.

Each person will have different types of expenses so it's important to remember everything you spend each week and budget accordingly. Put that amount into this account. If you run out of money in this account one week RESIST the temptation to dig into your other accounts. GO WITHOUT! Be frugal! It's surprising how much you can do without when you have to!

There are plenty of online budget planners on the internet to help with this part of the plan or use our budget planner: -

http://advancedfinancialsolutions.smartonline.com.au/calculators/budget-planner/

If it becomes too difficult to work out by all means get the advice of a trusted financial planner, mortgage broker, accountant or us of course. The idea is to get help when you need it. You don't have to do this alone. There are experts out there to help and we are more than happy to help!

At this stage of the plan it's a great idea to tell your friends and family that you have decided to save for your home and that you are cutting back on your spending. That way if you usually buy them a $100 birthday present they won't be too shocked to receive a nice homemade card instead or surprised when you say no to social invitations. You might even inspire others to get on the bandwagon as well and join you!

If you are going to save for your deposit, it's a great time to get creative and think of ways of cutting back on your expenses to accelerate your savings plan.

My suggestions include: -

- Live out of your pantry for a week – the money you save that week on groceries can go into your home savings account.
- Look for specials whenever you do your grocery shopping – some of the home brand or generic items are just as good as the big name items and far cheaper
- Take your lunch to work every day and make your coffee/tea at the office instead of buying it at your local café on the way. Even better, give up the coffee and alcohol – that can save a lot of people a lot of money!
- Make a list when you go grocery shopping and stick to it – impulse items all add up and you don't need them.
- Don't go to the supermarket when you are hungry – you WILL buy more!
- Have a garage sale – it's surprising how much you can get for items you no longer want. Get rid of anything you haven't used in the last year. My best tip for garage sales is to have a sale of 3 items for $5 rather than selling things for $1 or $2 each – that way you are making at least $5 on each sale.
- Make homemade gifts and cards for friend's birthdays.
- Pick flowers from your garden to give as presents.
- Socialise in free locations such as picnics in the park or at the beach rather than in restaurants/bars/pubs.

- Organise a get-together with friends and take all of your pre-loved clothes, shoes and bags – swap for free. You might end up with a new favourite outfit without paying a cent!
- Ring your electricity company and negotiate a lower rate. I did this with mine about 2 years ago and got a 12% discount on the bill which really made a big difference. Do the same with your phone bill, insurance, health insurance, life insurance, etc. Go through all your bills and see what savings you can find.
- Instead of buying a new book ask friends if they have some you can swap
- Save on electricity – turn off and unplug all appliances you are not using and turn off lights in rooms you are not using.
- Change grocery stores. A few years ago I decided to try a different grocery store and ended up saving about $75 a week on our weekly bill – now that's a LOT of money!
- Join online communities/groups where people are sharing their money-saving ideas. There are some great ideas out there and people love to share their success stories
- Get an extra 2 weeks out of your next haircut and colour. If you get your hair cut and coloured every 8 weeks change it to every 10 weeks. That will save you the cost of around one haircut a year.
- Cancel your gym membership during the warmer months and exercise outside.

- If you are having friends over, ask everyone to bring a plate to share.

These all might seem like small ways to make a difference but trust me, the small steps all add up to making up the deposit. It might not happen as fast as you would ideally like but each time you save it will add up to the total over a period of time.

CHAPTER 3

YOU NEED A PLAN

It's so important to put a "home ownership" plan in place so that you have a goal to work towards and a "road-map" to help you get there.

I am a huge believer in goal setting to achieve your dreams.

I also love vision boards, visualization, positive affirmations and self-belief. These things are all important and will help make your dreams a reality.

One thing about finance is that action is the key to success and having a written plan to stick to can be a really big help.

A lot more people are successful in becoming homeowners if they have a plan, as opposed to just trying to save without any specific and measurable goals.

Case study

I had a lovely couple, Mick and Sarah, come and see me around 10 years ago. They wanted to buy their own home but had no savings. They wanted to know how much they would need to save, as well as checking what their borrowing capacity was, to make sure their goal was realistic.

We worked out how much they would need to save and then worked out a budget for them so they could achieve their goal.

Mick worked at our local school and Sarah was a receptionist at one of our local resorts. With our savings plan we calculated that it was going to take them approximately two years to get into their own home. Knowing this, made all the difference to them because suddenly their dream became real. Now they had an achievable goal that they could work towards within a planned time frame.

Prior to that appointment they had tried to save but things always came up and they kept digging into their savings for everyday items and lifestyle choices.

The result was that they fast-tracked their whole savings plan. Sarah took on extra shifts and Mick worked an extra day doing garden work on the weekends. Around 12 months after our first meeting Mick phoned me, sounding very excited – they had saved their deposit! They were over-the-moon. I'll never forget that phone call.

We got a pre-approval for the property and they found their dream home within weeks.

The day we received the formal approval, they snuck over the fence of the home that night, armed with a bottle of wine and were rolling around on the grass and laughing like excited kids at Christmas time.

Once they had moved in, they said one of the things they loved the most was being able to put nails in the walls to hang pictures without having to ask the landlord's permission. It's these types of stories that make me love what I do. ☺

SO REMEMBER: YOU NEED A PLAN. And getting an effective plan together is a lot easier if you have the right help and support.

I wouldn't try and service my car because I am not a mechanic. Similarly, it makes sense for anyone who doesn't work in finance to approach an expert while making one of the biggest decisions of their lives. So, if necessary, find yourself a good mortgage broker or financial planner to help develop the right plan for you.

Make sure your plan covers these 4 important points: -

1. Work out how much deposit you need to save
2. Work out how long it will take you to save this amount
3. Put together a budget
4. Set up your 3 savings accounts to get started.

Remember – every cent counts and you need to start somewhere. It won't always happen quickly but there is a good old saying about slow and steady wins the race. Even if it takes a few years it will still be worth it!

Review your budget/plan every 6 months to see if you are on track, and whether there are any improvements that can be made to fast track your plan.

Once the plan is in place don't be at all surprised if you achieve your goals faster than you expect!

CHAPTER 4

FIRST HOME OWNERS GRANT

The First Home Owners Grant is a government grant generally available for Australian permanent residents or citizens (aged 18 and above) who are buying or building their first home. It is available to individuals only, i.e. not companies or trusts. You must be planning on living in the home within 12 months of buying it and, in most cases, you must be planning on living in the home for at least 6 continuous months. Usually applicants and their spouses must not have owned property before to qualify for the grant.

Case Study

I had a young couple, Maree and John, who came to see me in April 2013. They were planning on buying their own home for around $450,000 but were unaware of the grants available.

When we discussed their options they soon realised that by buying a brand new house/land package they only needed about half the amount of savings than they would have needed to buy an already established older home.

They bought a very reasonably priced block of land for $200k, which was small (but in the area they liked) and put a lovely 4-bedroom home on the land for $230k on a fixed price contract. This meant they qualified for exemption from stamp duty on the purchase AND they qualified for the First Home Owners Grant, which was $15k at the time. A great saving for them! ☺

In this instance they required a deposit of $22,000 to get a loan approval through on the $430,000 house/land package - they paid no stamp duty and they received $15,000 from the NSW Government through the First Home Owners Grant. In contrast, if they had bought an established home for $430,000 they would have required a deposit of around $43,000 deposit and wouldn't have received the grant.

The availability of First Home Owner Grants varies from state to state in Australia and changes frequently.

Full details of the grants available in each state can be found at the following link:

http://www.firsthome.gov.au/

In NSW (for example) if you are buying your first home and the property is either:

- Land and construction (so buying land and building a house)
- A brand new home, duplex or townhouse (never lived in)
- Has a purchase price/value under $750k

This could mean you qualify for the First Home Owner (new home) Grant of $10,000.

In addition to this, you could also be exempt from stamp duty on the purchase. Check with your solicitor or conveyancer on this as the amounts change on a regular basis.

All of this adds up to substantial savings!

It is definitely worth checking out what grants are available as they can dramatically reduce the deposit required to buy your own home.

Please check the above information at the time of reading as these grants and exemptions change quite regularly.

CHAPTER 5

THE VISION – TO LIVE IN YOUR DREAM HOME

It's important to have a clear vision of a home you would not only love to live in but also one that you can afford.

In other words, there is no point in visualizing a residence that is going to be way out of your price range.

So, in order to do this, you need to jump onto the internet and do some searching. Some of my favourite sites for this are www.realestate.com.au or www.domain.com.au. Have a really good look around.

Check out the types of homes you like in the areas you would like to live in and make sure the prices are within your reach.

For your first home it's often better to start off with a cheaper home or even one that you could do some renovations on.

If the price is a little cheaper the time frame to achieve your dream will be shorter.

Case Study

One of the first loans I organised was for a client, Sue, who had split up with her ex-husband and was now living on her own. They had sold their home and she was miserable renting. There were lots of things wrong with the property she was living in and the landlord was not very prompt in getting the repairs done. She found the idea of taking out a mortgage on her own completely overwhelming but she had been referred to me by a friend so she decided to come in and discuss her borrowing capacity and options.

The first thing I pointed out was that the payments on her rental were almost the same as the repayments on a mortgage would be. So nothing would change with the amount of money going out weekly – except of course that she would be paying off her own home instead of someone else's. She easily qualified for a loan so we started to have a look on the internet at homes available in her price range. Once she saw that it was possible for her to buy a gorgeous home of her own she got really excited and her fears melted away. Often the vision of the property is all you need to get excited and motivated. ☺

Find a home you would love to live in and really IMAGINE yourself living there. A good way to do this is to cut out (or print) pictures of the house and stick them in a journal, or on a vision board or on your fridge. Every time you look at those photos you can reaffirm to yourself that one day soon that will be your home.

CHAPTER 6

HOW MUCH DEPOSIT DO YOU NEED?

So now you have an idea of approximately how much your future home is going to cost.

The next thing you need to do is work out how much the deposit will have to be.

The larger the deposit you have the less you will pay in fees, plus you will look more attractive to a bank with a large deposit.

Most lenders require a 5% deposit on the home, as well as another 5%-8% of the purchase price to cover the other costs involved with buying a home such as:

- – Stamp duty
- – Legal fees
- – Title search and registration fees
- – Pest and building inspection
- – Strata report
- – Insurance on the home
- – The list goes on

This varies from state to state/territory because each state and territory has different stamp duties and transfer fees so just use the figures I am giving you below as a guide. I strongly suggest making an appointment with a mortgage broker to get a more accurate figure so you know exactly what you are aiming for.

In most states/territories it usually works out to be approximately a combined total needed of around 10%-13% of the purchase price on an established property, although of course this varies depending on the lender too so just use this figure as a guide.

If you are buying a brand new property, the deposit and costs needed will usually be around 6% of the purchase price due to concessions on stamp duty and the First Home Owner's Grant. Once again this is going to vary depending on which state or territory you are in and also depending on which lender you are using so just use this figure as a guide.

So, for example, if you want to buy a home for $350k you are going to need an absolute minimum of $35,000 for an established home (in most states) or a minimum of $21,000 for a brand new property.

If you want to buy a home for $400k you are going to need a minimum of around $40k in savings or $24,000 for a brand new property (on average).

The more deposit you have the better as the lenders all love a large deposit and the lower amount you will pay in LMI.

CHAPTER 7

LMI – WHAT IS IT?

LMI stands for Lenders Mortgage Insurance.

Almost everyone wants to be able to buy a home with the smallest deposit possible.

Lenders Mortgage Insurance (LMI) is an insurance that allows you to achieve the dream of home ownership without having a 20% deposit (plus costs) which is required by the banks/lenders to avoid LMI.

If you have less than a 20% deposit in most cases you will be required to take out LMI to enable you to borrow enough to buy your home.

LMI is an insurance that allows you to borrow more than 80% of the purchase price of a property. **It covers the bank** if you don't make the payments on the loan. Therefore, it reduces the bank's risk in giving you the home loan. It is a one-off premium (so not payable each year – just a one-off insurance premium paid at the time of the loan settlement).

Most lenders will allow you to add some (if not all) of this insurance premium to the loan amount, so that way it is built into the home loan repayments over the full term of the loan.

At the moment most lenders will let you borrow 95% of the purchase price of an owner occupied property and add most (if not all) of the LMI to the loan amount.

The premium of the LMI and the amount the lender will add to the loan varies from lender to lender so it can prove rather confusing. There are plenty of online calculators which will give you a rough idea as to the amount of the LMI premium but I feel you are better off asking a broker or your lender to work this out for you as it's a very confusing part of the home loan process.

The lender will organise the LMI at the time of the loan approval. LMI is NOT TO BE confused with personal insurances such as income protection, life insurance, trauma, etc. LMI covers the lender (not you).

CHAPTER 8

WHAT MAKES A DEPOSIT ACCEPTABLE TO THE BANK?

OK, so let's consider for a moment the sort of deposits that banks approve of.

If you have less than 20% deposit plus enough to cover stamp duty, legal fees, etc. then most of the time the banks require you to save up the deposit over a period of at least 3 months. This enables them to see that you are able to save over a period of time and have responsible saving/spending habits during that time.

Savings held in your account for at least 3 months are called "genuine savings" and the lenders all love "genuine savings".

If you are being gifted the deposit (depending on the amount you are being gifted) they may also need these funds to sit in your account for at least 3 months to prove that you can leave them in your account untouched for at least 3 months.

If you are renting through a licensed real estate agent and can show 12 months of on time rental history - and you have at least 10% of the purchase price in savings – then with some lenders the funds don't need to sit in your account for more than a day! Ask your agent for a copy of your rental ledger to prove this. A lotto win would work well here – ha, ha! I had a client win $70,000 in Powerball once and had their deposit saved overnight! ☺

Remember to consider the possibility of a family pledge or family gift (Chapter 1 for more information).

If you have no choice but to save madly for your deposit, then work out how long it's going to take you to get your deposit together. This will give you a schedule and a goal to work towards.

Once you have your deposit you will have achieved the all-important first step!

CHAPTER 9

BORROWING CAPACITY

All lenders have different borrowing capacities which is why you might qualify with one lender but not with another.

When they are working out your borrowing capacity they take into consideration your income, living expenses, number of dependent children, repayments on any existing loans, regular outgoings such as child maintenance or HECS and the LIMITS on your credit cards.

For example, a couple earning $30,000 each with no dependent children and a $3,000 credit card limit could possibly borrow up to $429k (on average). ** This figure changes from lender to lender and depending on living expenses and rates at the time of application but this will give you a rough idea. **

If you want to have a play around with your borrowing capacity, try the calculator in the link below. The interest rate it defaults to is possibly not the correct rate so check the rate and change which will give you a more accurate figure:

http://advancedfinancialsolutions.smartonline.com.au/
calculators/borrowing-power-calculator/

Just use the figures as a guide. Interest rates change all the
time and so do the lenders' servicing calculators. So, for a
more accurate figure, I recommend an appointment with
your mortgage broker to discuss your borrowing capacity
and they can compare a range of lenders for you. We invite
you to contact us for this service - Ph 0249 190 478.

CHAPTER 10

WHAT DO LENDERS ACCEPT AS "INCOME"?

Ok, so we've looked at the deposit and savings aspect of getting into your new home. The next thing we need to discuss is "income".

In the eyes of MOST lenders they will accept any of the following as income:

- – Full time
- – Part time
- – Casual (some lenders prefer at least 12 months in a casual position - some prefer even longer. However, in most cases, 6 months is long enough)
- – Family Assistance Part A
- – Family Assistance Part B
- – Pensions (carers, veteran's affairs, etc.)
- – Rental income
- – Self-employed taxable income - as well as some expenses which can be added back into the income

There are other incomes that the mainstream lenders won't accept but a few of the smaller non-conforming lenders consider to be acceptable. These include foster care income, Newstart, and single parent pensions.

If you are self-employed the lenders ideally like 2 years of financials to show your income. However, there are a few lenders that will accept one full year of tax returns and tax assessment notices.

CHAPTER 11

LOAN REPAYMENTS

So now that you know what your borrowing capacity is (in the bank's eyes) it's time for you to seriously consider whether you can afford the repayments.

The banks work out your borrowing capacity based on your living expenses and existing debts but some people spend more than the average amounts that are used in the calculations. So you need to look carefully at your income and spending and make sure you can afford the payments once the loan is in place.

As an example, a $400,000 loan would be about $456 per week. Can you afford the repayments?

If you would like to play around with loan repayments and amounts, click on the link to the following calculator. The interest rate defaults to 5.5% p.a. so just change that to 4% p.a. for the purpose of the exercise. That interest rate will depend on the lender and what rates are doing at the time but it will give you a rough guide for now.

http://advancedfinancialsolutions.smartonline.com.au/
calculators/loan-repayment-calculator/

Your mortgage broker or lender can give you a more accurate
figure.

Once you know what the payments will be, you can compare
this amount with what you are currently paying in rent plus
the amount you are able to save. This will give you a good
indication of whether your loan is affordable or not.

CHAPTER 12

LOOKING APPEALING
TO LENDERS

Love is in the air today so I thought I would give you some tips about how to look fabulous in the eyes of the banks.

It's important to keep in mind that the person assessing your loan application has absolutely no idea who you are or anything about you. They don't know if you are a good credit risk or a bad one so they are going to analyse the information you give them carefully to make an informed decision about whether they should approve your loan application or decline your loan application.

The more information you can give to your broker or lender to assist with the assessor's decision making the better.

Here are some tips: -

1. Always pay your rent on time and when applying for a loan, supply a copy of your rental ledger for the

past 6–12 months. They love to see you are capable of paying on time. Your real estate agent can give you a copy of your rental ledger. If you are renting privately get a copy of the lease agreement and a statement to show where the payments are coming out of your account.

2. Have a separate savings account that you don't touch for at least 3 months. Add to it but don't make any withdrawals. The banks love to see that you can live without digging into your savings. They consider this to be genuine savings.

3. Reduce the limits on your credit cards. The banks take into consideration the full limit on all your credit cards - so if you have some that you don't use, contact the bank and cancel the card or reduce the limit down as low as possible.

4. Pay all your bills, including phone bills, on time. If you have a dispute with a credit provider or phone company, make sure you still pay the bill on time because they may put a default on your credit rating if you are more than 60 days overdue.

5. If you sometimes work overtime, make sure you do a lot of it in the weeks or months leading up to the application. This will enable the banks to see what sort of income you are capable of earning. They will still work on the average overtime income you have earned in the previous year but it helps if you can show them what you are able to earn.

6. If you are self-employed make sure you declare your full income. If you make your income too low on paper the banks won't approve your application.

7. Gone are the days when you went into the bank in a suit and applied for the loan with the local bank manager who approved the loan. However, I do feel it's important to present yourself in a professional manner when going into the bank or for your appointment with your broker. Your character is often judged at first sight.

Documents you will need to take to the loan application interview are:-

If you are on wages:

- Identification – ideally driver's licence and birth certificate or passport
- 3 pay slips
- Copy of your most recent group certificate
- Copy of 3 months' statements on each and every bank account you have
- Copy of 3 months statements on any loans or credit cards you have
- Copy of your superannuation statement
- Copy of any life and income protection insurance you have

If you are self-employed:

- Identification – ideally driver's licence and birth certificate or passport
- 3 pay slips
- Copy of your last 2 years tax returns
- Copy of your last 2 years tax assessment notices

- Copy of 3 months statements on your business account
- Copy of 3 months statements on your personal savings accounts
- Copy of 3 months statements on any loans or credit cards you have
- Copy of your superannuation statement
- Copy of any life and income protection insurance you have

It's also advisable to take anything else that will give the lender or broker information about your financial position. Once again keep in mind that the assessor knows nothing about you so the documents you provide are what will be used to make a decision on the loan.

CHAPTER 13

SELF-EMPLOYED APPLICANTS

Who is considered to be self-employed? It can be: -

- anyone with their own business
- anyone with an ABN
- anyone who is a director of a company
- anyone that uses an ABN to contract to their employer rather than receiving wages/super
- anyone that gets wages but has any of the above as well

So, if you are employed by someone else on wages AND you are a director of another company you will need to provide taxation records for the past 2 years for your company as they need to assess your entire financial position as part of the loan application.

Self-employed applications can be a little tricky and the lenders are a little extra stringent on self-employed applications so you might find you are jumping through a few more hoops if you are self-employed. A lot of businesses fail so the lenders prefer to approve loans for business applicants who can show a good strong history of working in the industry plus positive income figures for the past few years.

A lot of self-employed people try and keep their taxable income as low as possible so that they are not paying too much tax but that won't help when you go to apply for a loan because the lenders do like to see enough income to cover living expenses and the loan repayments at the very least.

A good accountant will know how to give you the best of both worlds and claim deductions that the lender will add back into the taxable income which can help achieve the result you are after without having to pay too much tax.

If you are planning on applying for a home loan and you are self-employed I would suggest an appointment with a mortgage broker at least 12–18 months in advance to work out the minimum income the lenders require for you to achieve a loan approval for your ideal home. That way you can aim to have your income high enough to get the home loan approved.

If you are self-employed (or use an ABN to contract to your employer), the lenders will usually require a minimum of 2 years' tax returns and tax assessment notices to prove your income. There are a few lenders that will use one year only if you have been in the industry for at least 2-3 years.

Most lenders will base your income on your net taxable income plus most will add the following deductions:

- – Depreciation
- – Interest on any loans that are no longer in place
- – One-off expenses
- – Donations
- – Extra contributions to super

It's vitally important if you are self-employed that you use a good accountant that understands what the banks need to see when you are applying for a loan.

It can be very disappointing for clients who have made their income so low that they don't qualify for a home loan when their true figures (and paying a little more tax) would have achieved a different result.

Ideally, your income should be consistent or growing for the past few years. That will show the lender that your business is stable and growing. If there is a large difference between the past 2 years' income figures, then the lender will either use the lower of the figures or they will average the figures out. If you have had a big difference in income I suggest providing the lender with evidence surrounding the difference in the income. For example, I have a self-employed client who had consistent income for several years then a lower income for the most recent year because he spent quite a lot of money on new equipment in the business. This was considered a one-off expense and could be added back into the income. To prove this, we got a letter from his accountant and provided a copy of the invoice for the equipment.

If you are self-employed it's not a bad idea to give the lender an overview of your business and a short version of your business plan so that they can see your overall financial picture. The more positive information you can provide to the lender the more chance you have of getting an approval. Remember that the person assessing your loan doesn't know you at all so the more information you can provide to give them an overall picture of you the better.

CHAPTER 14

CREDIT REPORTS (PREVIOUSLY KNOWN AS "CREDIT RATING")

Often people get concerned about whether they need to have had a credit card or loan to give them a "good credit rating". This really isn't necessary.

A credit report shows your "credit history".

It will also contain your personal information such as: -

- Your personal information such as name, date of birth, current address, previous address and driver's licence number
- Your credit applications – usually for the past 5 years
- Repayment history
- Any poor credit history such as bankruptcy (up to 7 years), court judgements, defaults (up to 5 years)

Your credit report will show any applications you have made for loans, credit cards, store accounts, phone plans, interest free facilities, etc.

If you have some of these and you have paid them all on time, then that's wonderful. Your credit report will just show that you have applied for those facilities and that you have a "clean credit history".

If you HAVEN'T paid any of these on time and are more than 60 days late then it's quite likely you may have a DEFAULT listed on your credit report and that often makes it difficult to get finance. This is often referred to as a "bad credit rating".

There are lenders that will do loans for people with defaults, judgements and discharged bankrupt clients, so if you are in that position then all is not lost. However, a lot of the lenders will require a larger deposit and often the home loan will be a higher interest rate with higher set up fees.

It's very common for people to have a bad credit rating after changing addresses. They forget to notify the electrical provider or phone company which can lead to bills not being paid and a possible default on their credit rating.

It's recommended to check your credit report at least once a year because then if there are any issues on your credit report you can get them sorted out as quickly as possible, plus if there are any incorrect listings you can get them sorted out prior to applying for a home loan.

Want to know what YOUR credit report looks like? Most mortgage brokers can order a copy for you or you can order a copy online through many of the credit reporting agencies.

CHAPTER 15

WHAT TYPE OF HOME LOAN SHOULD YOU GET?

There are soooo many types of loans in the marketplace and this can make things extremely confusing! Some of the more common options available are:

– **Standard home loan** with a redraw facility. This is probably the most common type of loan taken by home buyers with one property as it usually has the lowest interest rate, set up fees, etc.

– **Offset home loan** - this is where you have an offset savings account which is linked to your home loan. Any money in your savings account is taken off the balance of the loan when the interest is calculated. So, for example, if you had a $400k home loan and you had $5k in your offset savings you would only pay interest on $395k. These are really popular with people who are paid monthly or have larger amounts of savings in their accounts on a regular basis.

- **Flyer Home Loan** - this is where you get Frequent Flyer points for taking out a home loan with the lender. This is popular for investors who don't mind paying a little bit more on the home loan interest rate because they know it will enable them to fly somewhere in the world for free. These loans often have a very slightly higher interest rate or an annual fee.

- **Revolving Line of Credit Home Loan** - this is where you have one gigantic limit on your home loan and when you make a payment on the loan the funds become available for you to use again down the track. I don't recommend these loans as it's like having a gigantic credit card which is tempting to never pay off.

CHAPTER 16

FIXED OR VARIABLE?

This is such a debatable subject. Rates are lower than ever at the moment (at the time of writing) but some of the economists are predicting one more rate reduction. Others are predicting that rates will stay the same for at least the next 18 months, while a few are even predicting that they may go up later this year.

With all this uncertainty, do you choose a fixed rate or variable or a combination of both?

The answer is different for every client.

The banks make a LOT of money out of fees associated with fixed rates so it's really important to know a few things about most fixed home loans:

- You can't pay more than $10k a year extra in payments without being penalised by most lenders
- If you pay extra you can't access the redraw on this until the fixed rate expires with most lenders

- You can't have an offset account with a fixed rate with most lenders
- If you sell the home or pay out the loan for any reason you will have a very high penalty for breaking the fixed rate term with most lenders

Some of the reasons you MIGHT choose a fixed rate would be:

- The security of knowing exactly what your rate is
- The security of knowing exactly what your repayments will be

Another option is to have a combination of fixed and variable. This is a popular option for people who want the security that comes with a fixed rate but also the flexibility to pay extra off the variable portion of the loan while still being able to access redraw and have an offset account.

If you are in any doubt at all I would suggest going with a variable rate because they are far more flexible than a fixed product and there are no hidden nasty exit fees for paying out a variable rate home loan.

CHAPTER 17

CHOOSING A LENDER

Choosing a lender can be very confusing.

Some lenders might have a very attractive interest rate but high set up fees, valuation fees, legal fees, ongoing fees or even hidden costs which are not widely advertised.

All of the fees associated with a loan need to be taken into consideration when working out the overall lender comparison rate (true rate).

The main lender fees associated with a home loan will be:

- Application fee (usually paid at the time of settlement not when you are applying for the loan)
- Valuation fee
- Legal fees
- Ongoing annual or monthly fee
- Lenders Mortgage Insurance (if you are borrowing more than 80% of the property valuation)

Often lenders will have specials which waive most of the above fees so it's really worth shopping around. Don't just go to wherever you bank because they might not be the most suitable choice for you!

It's almost impossible to choose a lender on your own and be sure you are getting a good deal - unless you are very well-informed on these matters.

This is why I highly recommend using a very experienced mortgage broker (I happen to know 3 great ones and they all work with me! ☺).

A good broker will compare many lenders, taking into consideration all the client's needs, as well as fees and charges. They will then present you with around 4 or 5 lender options to choose from with a detailed report about each one which will help you make an informed decision.

Most brokers don't charge a fee so there is usually no difference in using a broker or going directly to your bank/lender, but the advantage is you get their expertise to guide you through the process. Often they will help you understand the entire home buying process (not just the loan).

CHAPTER 18

PRE-APPROVAL

Once you have decided on your lender and loan type I highly recommend you do a pre-approval.

A pre-approval is an application for a home loan before you have found a property. These are sometimes called a conditional approval or home seeker loan.

A pre-approval means you put in a full application based on: -

- the price of a property you would ideally like to buy
- the loan amount you would require
- all the necessary supporting documents (pay slips, etc.)
- a "TO BE ADVISED" address.

The lender will then assess your application. It's quite common for them to come back and ask extra questions surrounding the application and once they are satisfied with the application and happy to approve a loan they will give you a "conditional approval" in writing.

The pre-approval lasts for around 3-6 months depending on the lender. This is usually enough time to find a property you would like to buy. If you haven't found a property by then the pre-approval will expire and you will need to re-apply but I would suggest not doing this until you are very serious about finding something because each time you apply and don't use a loan the application is registered on your credit report.

The advantages of pre-approvals are:

- It gives you confidence that you are going to be approved once you find a property
- You can show a real estate agent your pre-approval letter and they will then take your offers more seriously
- You are a few days ahead of other potential buyers when your offer is accepted

There is usually no charge for pre-approvals so they are a great way of ensuring your home loan would be approved and also a way of identifying any issues that may arise once you find a property to buy. It's better to get any issues ironed out in advance before you have found your dream home.

CHAPTER 19

LOANS FOR THE OVER 55'S

Ideally, you want to be applying for a home loan before you are 55 because once you've reached that age the lenders have to comply with an extra set of rules under the National Consumer Credit Protection Act 2009 (NCCP) responsible lending conduct obligations for consumer credit.

Most lenders want to ensure that you are able to have the loan paid up in full by the time you are 74. The reason behind this is that if you cannot pay the loan out by retirement age it could put you into financial hardship so the regulations are designed to protect you from an unsavory financial situation when you are no longer working.

Everything is not lost though. When we submit a home loan for someone over the age of 55 we submit a "full exit strategy" which shows the bank that our client can pay the loan out in full by the time they turn 74.

This might include things like: -

- – setting up the loan over a shorter loan term (instead of 30 years)
- – providing a copy of your superannuation showing the balance and how much you can pay off the loan once you retire
- – show assets that can be sold to pay lump sums off the loan

It's really important that this is done at the time of submitting an application for anyone applying for a home loan over 55 so that you increase your chance of approval.

Some lenders will consider downsizing an acceptable exit strategy, however, most won't so you need to show that you can pay the loan out in full so that you have no mortgage debt left by the time you retire. Ideally, that is what you want for yourself too as it would be very difficult to pay a home loan without wages.

CHAPTER 20

FIND YOUR HOME

Once you have the pre-approval in place, the next step is to find a property.

Hopefully you have been doing your homework so you can recognize a good buy when you see one.

It is vitally important to know exactly what you want so that when your dream home comes up it will feel right and you know that it's the right property for you.

Make a list of the things you MUST have and include: -

- – Suburbs
- – Minimum number of bedrooms
- – Type of home (freestanding house, townhouse, duplex, unit)
- – Minimum number of bathrooms
- – Type of garage and number of cars
- – Size of yard/land
- – Other essential features

Also include a list of "ideal features" that you would "ideally" have in your home but which are not essential such as: -

- 2nd living area
- Home office
- Fully fenced yard for the dog

Your list will be different to this but I'm sure you get the idea.

Once you have your "must have" and "ideal" lists I feel the best way to find a home is to contact a few good agents in your area and tell them what you are looking for. Meet with them in person so that you can really give them a good idea of what you are looking for. Give them your list. Once they know what you are after they can let you know as soon as they have a new listing (often before it goes onto the market).

You would be surprised at how many properties are sold before they are even listed or placed on websites. ☺

Once you have decided on a property I recommend that you choose a solicitor or conveyancer to handle the legal side of the transaction for you. You will need to let the agent know who you are using so that they can send the sales advice/contract through to them.

We also highly recommend that you get a pest and building inspection done on the property to ensure there are no issues with the property that you are not aware of.

CHAPTER 21

VALUATION

Once you have found your home, the bank/lender requires a copy of the contract of sale and then a valuation is done on the property by their own valuer or a panel valuer appointed by the bank/lender.

A bank valuation on your home is an essential part of the home loan process.

Once the bank has appointed a valuer to assess your property they will do a report for the bank based on: -

- – Location of the property
- – Number of bedrooms
- – Number of bathrooms
- – Number of other rooms
- – Type of car spaces
- – The condition of the property and its grounds
- – The structure and what the property is made out of
- – The age of the property
- – The zoning

- Recent comparable sales in the area
- Any market conditions or risks that could affect the future value of the home or the area

There are a number of types of valuations ordered by the bank which include:

1. Full Valuation – this is where a valuer goes to the property and inspects the property inside and out.
2. Kerbside Valuation – this is where the valuer goes to the property but assesses the property from the outside of the property.
3. Desktop Valuation
4. Construction Valuation – this is where the valuer will determine the value of the land and the home you are building to determine the value of the home upon completion of the construction.
5. Off the Plan – this is where the valuer will determine the value of a property once the property has been completed.

In most instances, the valuer will value the property at the contract price unless they feel you are paying too much for the property. Most valuers are of the opinion that what a client is prepared to pay for a home is what it is worth, so in 99% of cases the valuation comes in at the price you are paying.

If the valuation comes back at the price you are paying you can get some comfort in the fact that the valuer doesn't feel you are paying too much for the property.

If the valuation comes in at a different price than what you are paying then the lender will use the lower of the two figures as the value on the home. So if the valuation comes in lower than the contract price, the loan amount MAY be reduced down accordingly (depending on what percentage you are borrowing). However, it's very rare for a valuer to value a property less than the purchase price when they are valuing for a client buying a home. The price you are willing to pay generally determines the value. If your valuation does come in lower than the price you are paying I would strongly suggest doing some research into the reason why. Perhaps you are paying too much?

Valuations normally come back within 3-4 working days of being ordered.

The report will generally go back to the lender or your mortgage broker. Depending on the lender, a copy can sometimes be provided to you for your own records.

CHAPTER 22

LENDERS MORTGAGE INSURANCE APPROVAL

Once your valuation is back, the next stage is getting approval from LMI (lenders mortgage insurance) and then final approval from the lender.

Some lenders have their own internal sign off on the LMI approval (which means the loans assessor or someone internally within the bank can approve the loan on behalf of the mortgage insurer) and others have to have the loan approved by the mortgage insurer themselves.

The time frame on this stage of the application can vary from lender to lender and is anything from a few hours to a few days. Your mortgage broker or lender can give you an idea of the current turnaround times so you know what to expect.

This stage of the loan can be a little frustrating because often the mortgage insurer asks for further information about the client - so it is quite common to be asked for updated pay slips, bank statements or anything else they feel is relevant to your financial situation.

Some of our clients joke at this stage asking, "What are they going to ask for next? What I had for breakfast??" My answer is usually "No, but they might want to know the colour of your undies!" ☺

The best way to get through this stage is to keep providing them with anything they ask for. The fact that they are asking for more information is a good indication that they are almost certainly not going to decline an application. They very rarely ask clients for more information then decline an application, so try and see this as a positive sign. You just have to keep jumping through those hoops!

CHAPTER 23

FORMAL APPROVAL

The bank issues a formal approval in writing.

This is sometimes called an unconditional approval or comfort letter.

This means that you now have a full approval and there are no more conditions or documents that the bank/lender needs to see prior to approving your loan.

It's usually a big relief for everyone when this letter arrives as it means you have successfully jumped through all the necessary hoops.

A formal approval is usually a one-page letter on letterhead from the lender confirming basic loan details such as: -

- – Your details
- – The loan amount
- – The interest rate
- – The property being used as security

It's important to check the details in the letter carefully as sometimes the lender will change the loan amount at formal approval stage and occasionally errors are made. It's better to double check the figures now rather than find out at settlement that you haven't borrowed enough!

Once you are happy with the details in the formal approval it needs to be sent to your solicitor or conveyancer.

It is VITALLY important that they go through the approximate settlement costs with you to make sure that the combined total of your loan and savings is enough to complete the purchase.

You don't want to get to settlement day and not have enough money.

Brokers and lenders can also go over the approximate costs with you but this step really needs to be done by a legal person to get more accurate figures.

CHAPTER 24

LOAN DOCUMENTS

Once your formal approval is issued, loan documents are sent out.

Each lender has a different system for this. Some will send them to your local branch of the bank, some will send them to your broker, some will send them to your solicitor and some will send them directly to you. They usually have signature tabs so you know where you need to sign.

Before signing, it's imperative to have the loan documents explained by someone that understands the documents (such as your mortgage broker or your solicitor/conveyancer) because they can be very confusing and it's obviously VERY important to understand what you are signing.

Documents that are normally included will be: -

The Loan Contract – this is a formal letter of offer from the lender to you. This will be issued with the lender's terms and conditions of the mortgage. It is vitally important that you understand this document. This document will have the interest rate, the term of the loan along with the fees and charges associated with the loan, as well as any future fees and charges which may be charged to the loan at a later date. The fees and charges section of this document can be very confusing as the lenders are required to list absolutely all possible fees associated with their home loans and a lot of them may not be applicable to you. Once again I strongly suggest you get a qualified mortgage broker or your legal representative to go through these documents with you.

The Mortgage Document – this is the legal document that is lodged by your lender with the relevant state or territory to register the mortgage on the property. It is used in the mortgage registration process by the lender. This document must be signed by you and witnessed

Witness Document – most lenders have a document that is required to be completed by the witness confirming that they saw you witness the form and that they personally know you or have sighted your identification to confirm your legal identity. Often copies of your identification need to be returned with the witness document.

Settlement and Disbursement Form – this document will give instructions to the lender on where you want any surplus funds or any extra funds to come from to make up the settlement. It may also have a section in the form where you can authorize your solicitor to instruct the bank/lender on your behalf.

Loan Payment Authority – some lenders will send this form out so that payments can be set up by the lender as soon as settlement takes place. This form will ask you how often you want to make payments on the loan and where you want the payments to come from.

You cannot make any changes to the mortgage documents so if you make a mistake you will need to get the documents reprinted. Don't use any liquid paper or white out to fix mistakes. Alterations are not permitted on loan documents.

At this point in time we also suggest organising insurance on the property. You will need to have insurance organised on the home before settlement. It could also be a good time to do a review of your life insurance, income protection insurance, trauma insurance and also update your wills. This is just covering all bases and part of responsible lending.

CHAPTER 25

READY FOR SETTLEMENT

Once you have signed your loan documents and returned them to the lender they will check the documents to ensure that you have signed everything correctly and that all your documentation is now in place.

This is an important part of the process because incorrect documents could cause a delay in your settlement.

If there are any documents that have not been returned and signed correctly the lender will re-issue the document for you to sign. It will be vitally important to send the document back as quickly as possible to avoid any delays in your home settlement taking place.

Once all the checks have been done on the documents the lender will certify your file as "Ready for Settlement".

The lender will send your solicitor or conveyancer a "ready to book" advice statement. This is usually sent via fax or email from the lender or their settlement agent advising your solicitor or conveyancer of the following information: -

- Your file number
- The amount of funds available from your loan for settlement
- Contact information for making the settlement booking
- Settlement booking instructions
- Any special requirements for the settlement to take place

This means that the loan is now ready for a settlement booking and the date of the settlement can be booked and confirmed by your solicitor or conveyancer.

From here your solicitor or conveyancer takes over and organises the settlement to take place.

They will usually: -

- Co-ordinate the settlement date, time and location with the seller's solicitor or conveyancer
- Co-ordinate the settlement date, time and location with your lender
- Prepare all the required legal documents for settlement
- Work out settlement figures and cheques or extra payments required

They will advise you of the settlement date and also give you instructions on how they want any extra funds required to be paid.

The settlement is when all of the documents and money are handed over between the vendor (seller), you and any banks or lenders involved in the transaction.

Each solicitor/conveyancer does things slightly different so it will be important for you to check what they need from you prior to settlement.

CHAPTER 26

SETTLEMENT DAY

We are on the home stretch now! It's settlement day.

It's a good idea for you to do a final inspection of the property this morning (or as close to today as possible) to ensure that the property is still in the same condition as when you purchased it, and that it has been left in a reasonable condition. Also check that any items that were to remain in the home have been left behind by the sellers in a reasonable condition. If there is anything you are concerned about contact your solicitor immediately.

Your solicitor or conveyancer will attend settlement on your behalf and then let you know once it has taken place.

This happens at a location and time agreed upon by all parties. Some settlements are now done online using an online exchange system and I do believe this system will continue to grow in Australia.

People that attend the settlement are usually: -

- Your solicitor or conveyancer
- The vendor's (sellers) solicitor or conveyancer
- Any banks or lenders that have an interest in the transaction. (This will usually be your lender along with the vendor's lender if they have an existing mortgage on the property)

In most cases you don't personally attend the settlement. It's a meeting between the legal representatives of the seller and the buyer along with any lenders who have a registered interest in the property.

During settlement the legal representatives usually: -

- Hand over the relevant legal documents
- Hand over any cheques or settlement funds

Once settlement takes place your solicitor or conveyancer will usually call you to confirm that settlement has taken place and they will email or fax the real estate agent to confirm settlement.

Once settlement has taken place you can pick up the keys to your new home!

A very exciting day!

CHAPTER 27

CONGRATULATIONS!!

AFTER SETTLEMENT TAKES PLACE YOU ARE A HOME OWNER - YOU HAVE ACHIEVED THE DREAM!

This is not where the story ends though as you are now the proud owner of a home loan (mortgage).

I highly recommend that you now go into the branch of the lender with your broker (or call the lender if you have used an online home loan) and set up the following: -

- Internet banking access so you can view your home loan online
- Organise your pay to start going into that bank/lender- it's much easier if you have all of your banking with the same financial institution as your home loan
- Transaction cards for any savings accounts that you opened as part of the home loan (usually a debit VISA or MasterCard)

- Organise automatic home loan payments to come out so that you don't need to make the payments manually each time they are due

I suggest you pay your home loan payments on a weekly or fortnightly basis (whenever you are paid). You should start to make your home loan payments straight away. Most lenders will allow you to make the payments weekly, fortnightly or monthly.

You will have a minimum payment required but with most lenders you can also pay extra if you want to. If you do pay extra, in most cases you will be able to redraw back those extra funds if you need it down the track. Check the conditions of redraw on your specific loan type though just to be sure.

NOW YOU CAN CELEBRATE!!

Take time to enjoy your new home and celebrate your success. Perhaps a housewarming party? (Don't forget to ask everyone to bring a plate! ☺).

I hope you find the time to share the information in this book as well as your own story. This may inspire others to achieve their dream of owning their own home.

CONCLUSION

I sincerely hope this information has helped you understand the process of applying for finance and buying your first home. If you would like any further information, please do phone or email me.

It truly is my passion to get as many Australians into their own homes as possible - so please feel free to make an appointment with me or one of my amazing team (in person, Skype or over the phone).

We will then get your plan in place and launch you on the road to owning your own home.

Ph. 0249190478 or anita@advancedfinance.com.au.
My website address is www.advancedfinance.com.au
We can also be found on Facebook – www.facebook.com/advancedfinance

Anita Marshall

DISCLAIMER

At the time of writing this book (August 2016) the information in this book was accurate, however, because of the highly evolving rate of the finance and real estate industries, Anita Marshall and Advanced Finance Solutions will endeavour to update this book as needed. However, information can change without notice.

We do not guarantee the accuracy of information in the book at any particular time.

Every effort has been made to ensure that the information provided is accurate.

Individuals must not rely on this information to make financial or investment decisions. This information is general in nature only. Before making any financial decisions, we recommend you consult a mortgage broker, financial planner and accountant to take into account your particular investment objectives, financial situation and individual needs to consider if the information contained within this book is appropriate for you.

ABOUT THE AUTHOR

Anita Marshall

Anita Marshall's mission is to help Australians get out of the rental market and into their own homes by motivating and inspiring others to achieve what she has done for herself and many of her clients.

Anita is the Managing Director of Advanced Finance Solutions (mortgage brokers) so her personal experiences and that of her clients has given her a wealth of information which she loves to share with potential home buyers.

She is also proud to be one of the published authors in the best-selling books "Ignite Your Investment Property

Mojo", "The Path To Success" (which is full of inspirational stories from entrepreneurs around the world including Dr Wayne Dyer, Brian Tracy, Arielle Ford and Sandy Forster), and "Sprout The Life You Love" which is a compilation book full of tales and secrets from Female Entrepreneurs including Rhonda Britten and Poppy King.

Anita holds a Diploma in Mortgage Broking, Certificate IV in Mortgage Broking, Certificate IV in Financial Services, Diploma in Financial Planning and an Advanced Diploma in Business Management.

Anita is really passionate about helping Australians achieve the dream of owning their own homes.

Anita lives in Port Stephens with her son, Blake, and 3 dogs, Casper, Lola and Kash. Her parents, David and Rhonda Henry, live nearby. ☺

Printed in the United States
by Bookmasters